A BABY'S
MEMORY JOURNAL

Love • Record • Treasure Forever

Hardie Grant

QUADRILLE

THIS JOURNAL CELEBRATES THE
ARRIVAL AND FIRST YEAR OF

_____

WITH LOVE FROM

_____

Baby's given name

Baby's birthday

Baby's place of birth

Baby's first home

Parent(s)

Other significant adults involved in your baby's life

Siblings / half/step siblings

IN ANTICIPATION OF
YOUR BABY'S ARRIVAL

When and how did you know you first wanted a baby?

Can you convey how deep the longing was for your baby?

Were there any life-changing steps you needed to take to begin the journey to become a parent?

How bumpy or smooth was the road to your baby's conception?

Describe what happened on the day you discovered you were going to become a parent.

What emotions did you experience when you understood you were going to become a parent?

Record reactions of your family members to your baby news.

What preparations did you have to make to your home to accommodate your baby?

YOUR BABY'S ARRIVAL

When was your baby born?

Where was your baby born?

Who was in the room when your baby was delivered?

Who were the people you would like to remember in assisting in the safe arrival of your baby?

Who was the first to visit you and your baby?

Can you remember the national or international news on the day your baby joined your family?

When your eyes first fell on your baby's face, what did you see?

Describe your immediate reactions to your new baby.

Did the day of your baby's arrival go as you had initially planned?

Were there elements of peril you had to navigate during the baby's delivery?

Were there any immediate health concerns that needed to be addressed after delivery?

ABOUT YOUR BABY

When did you know what your baby would be called?

When did you name your baby?

What does your baby's name(s) mean?

Has your baby been assigned a gender?

What is the pronoun you prefer to use with your baby?

What colour was your baby's hair at birth? Has it changed at all?

What colour are your baby's eyes?

How heavy was your baby?

What is your baby's blood type?

What is your baby's star sign?

What were your first words to your new baby?

Did your baby's first feed go as planned?

What unique characteristic did you first note about your new baby?

What was your baby's first outfit?

Were there any family mementos or gifts that were important for your new baby to receive?

Who first changed your new baby?

YOUR BABY AT HOME

How and where did you spend the first few precious days with your new baby?

Who else was supporting you and your baby at home?

What acts of kindness from family members or friends can you remember from this time?

Were there times during your baby's first few days that either you or your baby struggled?

How did you overcome any difficulties in the early days?

Where did your baby initially sleep?

Describe the moses basket, bassinet, cot or co-sleeping bed that your baby nestled into.

Did sleep come easily to your baby?

How did your baby like to be held?

Books, music or hot drinks? What did you rely on to get you through those early long, dark nights?

Write down the lyrics to the song or lullaby that most soothed your baby.

YOUR BABY AND THEIR WIDER FAMILY

Who was living in the home that your baby joined?

How would you describe the family unit your baby joined?

Who were the first members of your wider family to meet your baby?

Record reactions of family members to your new baby.

Are there family members no longer with you that you would have liked your baby to meet?

Describe any family fractures that were healed by the arrival of your new baby.

How did you mark the arrival of your baby into the family?

Is your baby growing up within a particular religion or moral framework?

What do you think is important to preserve and celebrate from your baby's heritage?

Which symbols and stories from your baby's culture do you think it's important your baby is introduced to?

Record family wisdom regarding babies that you have found useful.

Which music surrounds your baby at home?

Which language(s) is your baby growing up hearing at home?

How have significant adults outside your family helped inform how you are raising your baby?

Are there any organisations, agencies, charities or social media groups that have helped you care for your baby?

YOU AND YOUR BABY

When did your baby first smile in response to you?

Recall the feelings you experienced the first time you and your baby truly connected.

Describe a moment when you first experienced profound happiness with your baby.

Which part of your baby's face or body were you particularly drawn to?

Are you able to describe how your baby smelled?

Recall your early feeding routine with your baby. Did you have a favourite chair, watch a particular programme or listen to music during the feeds?

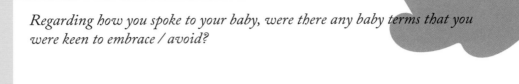

Regarding how you spoke to your baby, were there any baby terms that you were keen to embrace / avoid?

No sugar? Only organic? Describe your initial intentions in relation to raising your baby and how successful you were in keeping to them.

What do you feel you got right in those early months spent with your baby?

What aspect of early childcare did you find most challenging?

What has your baby taught you?

What elements of your lifestyle have you had to adapt to accommodate your baby?

Try to describe the love you feel for your baby.

YOUR BABY'S SOCIAL CIRCLE

Does your baby have a social media profile?

How did your community welcome your baby?

Outside of the family, who did you and your baby spend most time with?

Which other babies did your baby spend time with?

What baby groups did you attend?

Did you pro-actively make contact with parents in the same family situation as you and your baby?

Did your baby enjoy being in company or spending time quietly with fewer people?

Stick photographs here of your baby and their friends.

YOUR BABY GROWING UP

What did you love dressing your baby in?

Which baby outfit has a special meaning for you?

Did any particular colours suit your baby?

Did your baby self-discover a favourite blanket, cloth or soft toy?

When did your baby first laugh?

Recall bath times; what did your baby like or dislike about them?

Describe your baby's bedtime routine.

Using baby-safe ink, place your baby's hands and feet on these pages to make handprints and footprints.

What was the first book you regularly read to your baby?

What was the first nursery rhyme you sang to your baby?

Did your baby suck their thumb or fingers or self-soothe by any other method?

When did your baby begin sleeping through the night?

What did you enjoy doing after your baby had gone to bed for the night?

What noises did your baby make when they woke up?

When did your baby first roll over?

When did your baby first sit up unaided?

Stick photographs here of a special moment for your baby.

When did your baby grow their first tooth?

Were there any remedies you relied on for the teething period?

When was your baby first sick?

When did you begin weaning your baby?

What were the first foods your baby enjoyed?

Write down the recipe for your baby's favourite solid meal.

Were any ingredients you wanted to feed your baby difficult to find?

Describe the mess at your baby's meal times.

Were there any cafés you and your baby enjoyed visiting?

What were your baby's favourite foods for breakfast, lunch and dinner?

Stick photographs here of your baby enjoying their favourite meal.

Which toys did your baby seek out of its own accord?

Describe a regular walk you took with your baby.

What buggy / stroller / baby carrier did you use with your baby?

Were there special parks or gardens you and your baby frequented?

What caught your baby's eye when you went outside?

What animals did your baby like?

How old was your baby when they began to crawl?

When did your baby start playing by itself?

What games or baby equipment did your baby enjoy playing with?

What did your baby fixate upon?

Spell out your baby's first sound.

What was your baby's first word? Where was it uttered? What did it mean?

Record some words your baby used, understood only by you and your baby.

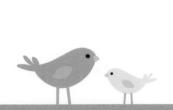

When did your baby first hurt themselves?

What did you worry about when your baby was very small?

Did your baby use a walker or any other device to help them toddle?

Set the scene for your baby's first steps.

Stick photographs here of a special moment for your baby.

Did your baby enjoy spending time outside?

Describe your baby's first pair of shoes.

When did your baby first enjoy a ride on a bus, train or aeroplane?

Have you and your baby had to travel far to visit any family members or significant adults?

YOUR BABY'S PERSONALITY

What would make your baby happy?

What would cause your baby to giggle?

What sensations did your baby most enjoy?

Where was your baby's most ticklish spot?

What would frighten your baby?

What would make your baby sad?

What would make your baby angry?

When did your baby first push you away?

Over which issues did your baby firmly and repeatedly shout 'NO'?

How would you soothe your baby?

Who else would your baby be happy to be soothed by?

Did your baby have a favourite colour?

Were there characters in books or online that your baby was particularly drawn to?

Describe your baby's emerging personality in three words.

Describe your baby's talents.

How would you describe your relationship with your baby?

Describe a perfectly ordinary but happy day spent with your baby.

HOPES FOR YOUR BABY'S FUTURE

Who are the role models, either within or outside your family, that you would like your baby to consider as they grow up?

Are there any golden rules that you would like to pass on to your baby?

What are the values you would like your baby to cherish?

What advice have you received that you would like to pass on to your baby?

What is the one thing about you that you would like your baby never to forget?

LETTER TO YOUR BABY

Write a letter to your baby filled with your hopes and dreams for their future.

BUSINESS DEVELOPMENT DIRECTOR Melanie Gray

EDITOR Stacey Cleworth

AUTHOR Joanna Gray

DESIGNER Katherine Keeble

HEAD OF PRODUCTION Stephen Lang

PRODUCTION CONTROLLER Sinead Hering

Published in 2020 by Quadrille,
an imprint of Hardie Grant Publishing

Quadrille
52–54 Southwark Street
London SE1 1UN
quadrille.com

ISBN 978 1 78713 573 4

Printed in China

FSC
www.fsc.org
MIX
Paper from
responsible sources
FSC® C020056